A hand-drawn town map with the following labels:

Legend:
1. St Mary's C...
2. Museum
3. Castle
4. Town Hall &
5. Corn Exchan...
6. Fry Art Galle...
7. Youth Hostel
8. The Priory
9. Methodist church

...church
...use
.... Council Offices
16. Police Station
17. Council Offices *
* weekend car parking

CW00411017

Streets and places:

Cambridge, Windmill Hill, Golf Course, Bridge End Gardens, Anglo American Playing Fields, Football Ground, CAR PARK, Upper, St..., Sheds Lane, Lt Walden Rd, Castle Street, Castle Hill, Ashdon Rd, Museum St., Bridge Street, Church Path, Church Street, Cockpit, Emson Close, Common Hill, THE COMMON, Chater's Hill, Hollyhock Rd, New Pond Lane, Freshwell Gdns, Freshwell Street, High St. North, Myddylton Pl., King St., Market Place, Butcher, Car Park, CAR PARK, 16, Maze, Radwinter Road, Haverhill, Park Lane, Mercer Row, Market Row, Hill St., East Street, New Road, Tanners Way, Farmadine, Thaxted Road, CAR PARK, SWAN MEADOW, Almshouses, Abbey Lane, Gibson Close, Gibson Way, High St. South, Gold St., George Street, Bandstand, Fairycroft Road, CAR PARK, Andley Road, South Road, Four Acres, Schools, Prospect Place, Hanover Place, Parkside, Battle Ditches, Gibson Gdns, Margaret Way, Andley Road, Station Street, Long Hedges, Farmadine Grove, Saxon Way, London Road, Debden Road, Station Road, Victoria Avenue, South Road, Chelmsford, Andley End Station, London Road, Newport Rd, Borough Lane, Little Larchmount, West Road

Compass: N, W, E, S

The parish church soaring above the town and girdled with trees, is the largest in Essex, built with the wealth from wool and saffron. Once considered for a cathedral, it watches over rather than dominates the houses below, some of whose roof tops are lower than the church's foundations. Despite its power in the life of the town, the independent, non-conforming character of its people was rich soil for the growth of Dissenters in the religious turbulence of the 17th century, especially of the Quakers. When persecution eventually ceased, their industry and initiative contributed largely to Walden's prosperity. There was also natural support for the Parliamentarians during the Civil War, for a brief period the town was the headquarters of General Fairfax and Cromwell himself when rather mutinous troops were camped in the surrounding countryside before the expedition to Ireland. There is, however, no record of a presentation of saffron to the Protector such as was made to both Charles I and Charles II when visiting Audley End!

History touched Walden lightly, but from its earliest years there was always the threat of invasion in time of war. Personal journals during the Napoleonic Wars speak of the preparations and training of the militia on the Common. In the First World War old people still remember the large white arrows painted on the walls, all pointing north for emergency evacuation – but no-one knew where to! The threat of course was most real in the 1939 war when Saffron Walden was in the Battle of Britain zone, with Debden, Duxford and other aerodromes in the near vicinity.

Thankfully, that invasion never occurred. Instead there was a friendly but troubled invasion of altogether two thousand evacuees from London and later by the American Air Force in great numbers. When the expected Germans came it was as young prisoners of war to a Hitler Youth Re-education Camp in a nearby village.

Small town though it is, Saffron Walden has always been proud of its Charters, the first dating to the early 13th century. Nor has it lacked men of eminence – an early Archbishop of Canterbury, two Lord Mayors of London, a prime minister to Queen Elizabeth I. This was Sir Thomas Smith, born of modest parentage, but whose great intellectual powers were early recognised. At the age of 13 he was studying at Cambridge University and throughout his life was a foremost scholar.

However, he is better known as a Tudor statesman, first as Secretary of State to the young Edward VI, but under Mary Tudor, as a strong Protestant, he returned to his scholar's life. Queen Elizabeth was to recall him as her Ambassador to

Castle

France and in later life he became her First Secretary of State. She appreciated his unswerving loyalty, although neither is said to have liked the other! Sir Thomas's dry way of recording the fact that he had come unscathed through the fires of Mary Tudor was his adoption of the salamander as his crest, replacing the eagle.

When Eddystone Lighthouse became automatic recently no man would have been more fascinated by the installation than Henry Winstanley, the Walden man who built the first Eddystone in 1696 and was lost when it was swept away in a violent storm five years later. This daring venture was the culmination of a lifetime of inventive and original undertakings. His designing talent was first recognised by Charles II when Winstanley worked as a youth at Audley End Palace as it was then known. Later he became famous in London and throughout Europe for his Water Theatre, based on a series of moving tableaux in which trick effects were achieved with fountains, water spouts and the mingling of fire and water. Winstanley's portrait hangs in the Museum and there still exist his engravings of Audley End as a vast palace. A shallow mound in nearby Littlebury marks the site of his fine house. He built it himself and it was so full of ingenious tricks and innovations that it became a legend in its own day.

One of the most colourful literary figures of Tudor times was Doctor Gabriel Harvey, son of a Walden ropemaker. A scholar, poet, Fellow of both Pembroke and Trinity at Cambridge and friend of the poet Edmund Spenser, he accumulated a great library in which his marginalia far exceeded his poetry in brilliance. He is most remembered for the long war of words he waged with Thomas Nashe, the dramatist, whose book *Have With You to Saffron Walden* is a vituperative attack on Harvey, ridiculing at one point his, 'grandiose oration to Queen Elizabeth' at Audley End. But sturdy Harvey outlived his attacker by thirty years, enjoying those years in retirement in his native town, and today *Have With You to Saffron Walden* is a happier bidding to which visitors from all over the world respond.

St. Mary the Virgin

Bridge Street

Late 15th century cottages. The heavy, narrowly spaced timbers indicate early building before oak became scarcer.

Although Saffron Walden was never one of the principal centres of the woollen industry in medieval times, it was a market town important enough to have its own Woolstaplers Hall, and the annual procession of the Woolstaplers on St. Blaize's Day (February 3) was a colourful occasion that was held until 1778 with the Mayor and Corporation taking part. Members of the Guild walked in their robes of wool dyed for the purpose, wearing feathered hats and led by a Bishop Blaize, their patron saint (who did not invent woolcombing as people believed but was an early Christian martyr tortured to death with woolcombs). Then came the chaplains, a band of music, shepherds and shepherdesses, one riding with a lamb in her lap. Orations were given at certain corners, and the procession even went beyond the boundaries of the parish as there were many weavers in surrounding villages. The church bells welcomed their return and they all feasted at the *Rose* (and *Crown*).

The traditional cloth woven in this neighbourhood was the 'white' or undyed type, although the town supplied the saffron dye for the whole area. It is also recorded that teazel, caraway and coriander

Weaver's Cottages

WEAVERS COTTAGES IN EAST STREET. A row of flint cottages with brick facings of the early 19th century built at the time of a revival of weaving.

WEAVERS COTTAGES IN GOLD STREET. 17th century cottages in a traditional weaving area, with a communal courtyard at the rear. Early 19th century prints show women stretching lengths of Norfolk crepe across the street.

were grown as a triple crop. The teazel, used for raising the nap on cloth is still to be found in gardens and hedgerows.

Although there was a general decline in the woollen industry weaving continued spasmodically and the spinning of worsted yarns was certainly being carried on here in 1823. There was also an unusual revival in the early 19th century with the introduction of Norfolk crepe weaving and there were as many as nine hundred looms busy in Walden and the villages, working for the factory at Bridge House. Cottages were built for weavers in East Street, Mt. Pleasant and Copt Hall. The Lord Braybrooke of that time deplored this industry which employed mostly young women, 'for the high wages led to idle and extravagant habits, so that the discontinuance of the work cannot be matter for regret'. His moral concern was soon to be satisfied and the day came when the last loom was silenced.

Maltings – Gold Street

Youth Hostel

GOLD STREET MALTINGS – The two-storey arched carriageway was specially constructed to admit laden wagons to the maltings and links the fine late 18th century house with the malting office.

MALTING INDUSTRY

Malting was carried on in Walden from the reign of Richard II. One reads of complaints even in 1372 of the tax demanded of one farthing on each quarter of malt bought or sold. In 1600 there were six maltings in the town; climate and soil here produced high quality barley suitable for making malt. By the end of the 19th century when London and other towns were expanding rapidly twenty-two maltings were operating and the record number of thirty-three was reached thirty years later. There was only one brewery in the town owned by the Gibsons, the leading maltsters, so all had to be transported to London.

Problems were too many for a command of the market to last – lack of water transport which nearby Bishop's Stortford could provide, heavy taxation, and the fact that the breweries began to cultivate their own supplies. So the decline followed that of wool and saffron, and the remarkable skyline of 'cowls rising up in all directions' began to disappear. Only ten maltings were left by 1901, but the sweet, heavy smell was to drift across the town for many years and one malting was still working after the last war. It has now been converted to a handsome printing press while retaining some external features.

YOUTH HOSTEL – The finest unspoilt medieval building in the town, early 16th century and used at an early date as a malting. The oak wheel sack hoist is still in position in a large dormitory open to the rafters. The building is L-shaped and on the side facing Myddylton Place are two original moulded oriels.

SAFFRON HARVEST

There is little beyond the name of the town to show that the delicate saffron flower once 'enamelled' the surrounding fields and was cultivated here for three hundred years. Eight little saffrons carved on the spandrel of an arch in the church, three on the coat of arms, others on the Charter of 1514 and the mace of 1685, and saffron patterns on pargetting, are all that can be traced.

On the other hand, the Town Libary is rich in the literature of a plant that was regarded as a remedy for ailments ranging from seasickness and jaundice to the plague itself – even recommended as an aphrodisiac. Top quality hay-saffron was reserved for the druggist; the lesser cake-saffron was used for dyeing and as an aromatic flavouring. The finest of course was always presented to visiting Royalty, often in a silver cup.

Tradition and the writer Hakluyt say that the first bulb, or corm, of Crocus Sativus was smuggled in the staff of a pilgrim returning from the Middle East. Though mentioned in the town records of 1444 as a tithable commodity, it is generally accepted that it was being grown a hundred years earlier. It needed the influence and promotion of that celebrated townsman, Sir Thomas Smyth to extend the cultivation and establish Walden as the most important saffron market in the country. Saffron also thrived as a crop here because soil conditions were ideal – temperate dry clay on a substratum of chalk. Only the necessary hot summers were sometimes lacking.

Preparations for planting were extensive and the Vicar of the nearby village of Radwinter, Rev. William Harrison, describes the cultivation, processing and cropping in Holinshed's Chronicle, 1587, with methods that varied little from those put forward by later writers. He said 'Warme nights, sweet dewes, fat grounds and misty mornings' were what saffron needed.

The flowers were picked in late September and the picking had all to be done by 11 am, or the blossoms wilted. Only the large stigmas, or 'chives' were kept and the discarded petals would fill the corners and alleys of the town, for 30,000 heads were needed to make five pounds of wet saffron, and one pound when dry.

The industry declined after 1725, had faded out by 1790 although one man was still taking his crop to London in 1820. Its demise had been hastened by the introduction of artificial dyes and cheap foreign imports. There was also less faith in its almost magical healing powers. The town has never been known for its 'Saffron cakes', so only the legend remains of what Nicholas Culpeper called 'an herb of the sun and under the lion . . . which strengthens the heart so exceedingly.'

WALDEN HOMES

Dragon Post - Youth Hostel

The Dragon post was frequently an inverted tree trunk, with the width and strength to support the cross beams and 'diagonal' beam of the upper storey. 'Dragon' is thought to be a corruption of 'diagonal'.

Houses of six centuries mingle comfortably throughout the long stretch of High Street and Bridge Street, like succeeding generations of an ancient family. Most of those in Bridge Street – where country meets town with such pleasing suddenness – remain with little alteration to their original timber framed and plastered walls, often with jettied upper storeys.

Where Bridge Street runs into the High is a vista to the east of the equally ancient Castle Street where modest houses of all shapes and sizes huddle close as if still seeking the old shelter of the castle walls. Once poor relations of the town, their unself-conscious charm has brought them a new life as more appreciative 'comers-in' to Walden choose them for homes.

Along the undulating High Street 18th century red brick and 19th century grey gault brick or stucco often mask houses of Tudor or earlier origin, such was Walden's propensity to modernise itself. Chimneys, roofs and a glimpse of the rear view of a house may give a clue to period, while the upper storey of a shop can be in curious contrast to its 20th century wares. Many buildings have remained as private houses because the High Street was never such an important shopping area as King Street and the Market Place, but lately the increasing demand for hotel and office premises has brought about a number of conversions.

Solid Victorian and Edwardian villas grew up southwards beyond the former railway station and the development of new houses up to the outbreak of war reflected the desire to live outside the old town centre. This continued for some years as Walden developed and new estates still spring up. At the same time there is a positive move to the centre again, and town houses, flats and sheltered housing for the elderly are tucked into every corner where formerly stood an old malting, disused workshop or large garden.

Even since the war Walden has lost old buildings that should never have been demolished, but much remains and there is growing awareness of the need to preserve an unusually fine heritage.

The central streets of the town contain a number of medieval hall houses, sometimes altered, divided or refaced over the centuries but possible to recognise by the basic design of the low central 'hall' flanked on each side by a higher gabled wing, often oversailing the lower storey. In one instance a 19th century road widening lopped off one gabled wing.

Walden is a town for a 'walkabout' because it is so compact. Every little path between houses – 'twitchells' old local people call them – is worth exploring for the unexpected vista it can reveal.

Cottages . Bridge End

Originally a 15th century yeoman's house, considerably altered in the 17th century. The interior still retains some original roof timbers, with a Tudor chimney inserted alongside the earlier kingpost.

Myddylton Place

An unusual cottage of 15th century origin, possibly an outbuilding developed later into a dwelling place. The apparent cul-de-sac of Myddylton Place leads through a 'twitchell' back into the High Street.

Early 15th century, previously adjoining a larger timber framed house which was dismantled and re-erected in West Grinstead, Sussex, in 1934. The spider window is an unusual feature.

The Close - High St.

A harmonious example of a house that 'grew' over the centuries. The central part of the house was built in the 16th century and associated both with Sir Thomas Smyth and William Holgate, friend of Shakespeare. The Priory was extended in the 17th century and the charming Venetian window over the main entrance was added in the 18th century. The whole house was brickfaced a hundred years later.

The Priory - Common Hill

The curve of Castle Street into Museum Street follows the line of the original Castle Bailey. The wide area at the junction was known as the City and the stocks stood here when they were moved from the Market Place.

Perhaps the most decorative building in the High Street with its moulded bressummer beam, the variety of pargetting and the ranges of small leaded windows which suggest an early weaver's house. The 20th century shop below is unobtrusive.

Army & Navy Stores

Cottages - Museum St.

Three cottages, once a 15th century house, also follow the line of the Castle Bailey into Museum Street. Their heavy projecting upper storeys are supported by curved brackets.

A row of 16th century cottages leading up to the church were once part of maltings. They were modernised after the last war. The gabled house was earlier but altered in succeeding centuries, the front part being added in the 18th.

Cottages - Church Path

Timber framed 16th century house, with a second wing added in the 18th century when it was refaced and the elaborate pendant barge-boards added.

The grey plastered frontage gives an austere appearance to this fine red-brick house of the late 18th century. Its perfect symmetry is a pleasure, and the delicate glazing bars of the upper windows were not sacrificed to large Victorian panes. On the small entrance door to the south are early Tudor carvings preserved with layers of paint.

7. High Street

73. High Street

An example of a 17th and 18th century house 'modernised' in Regency times with an elegant front extension and façade. It has been suggested that the top storey was also added later.

Remains of Doorway
Rose & Crown

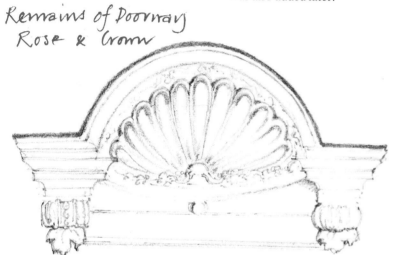

Early 19th century, bridging with dignity Regency restraint and Victorian heaviness. Originally a Gibson home, it has been for most of the 20th century occupied by local family doctors, and in recent years by solicitors.

53. High Street

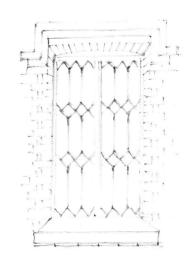

Window . 79 High Street

61, High Street

Detail of Window
61. High Sr.

Victorian Gothic boldly asserted itself in the High Street in 1860 with two lofty houses, bearing all the favourite features of the period – narrow lancet windows, church type doors, sharp gables and patterned bargeboards, clustered Tudor chimneys, even the ridge of the red and blue roof finished with ornamental cresting. Smaller versions of this type of house are scattered round the town and an even larger house on the outskirts was also built by this architect William Beck, who lies in the churchyard of the simple Saxon building at Strethall village.

The Common

The Maze

THE MAZE ON THE COMMON. Walden has open spaces of exceptional interest within short walking distance of the town centre. The passage between Boots and Barclays Bank in the Market Place leads directly to the Common, once Castle Green. Here in the shadow of the Castle in 1252 a Royal Tournament was held in which a Norman knight Ernulph de Monteney was slain, and over the centuries fairs, feasts, circuses and occasions of every kind have been centred here.

Near the eastern boundary is one of the finest rare earthen mazes in Europe, a quarter of a mile in circumference. Its true age has never been established as the date of 1699 for 'recutting' is the earliest mention in town records, but it is supposed to have replaced an earlier and larger one. The little brick path runs through its convolutions for nearly a mile before reaching the raised central island. And its early purpose – a Romano-British cursus for exercising soldiery? a penance by crawling for the pilgrim who turned back? We do know there was formerly a sportive game when young men had to run the narrow paths to compete for a girl on the island – or for a pot of ale!

BRIDGE END GARDENS. Walden in the 19th century was a town of large and beautiful gardens, three of them made by the Gibson family. Two of them are built over, but one belonging to their descendants, the Frys, is held by Saffron Walden on permanent long lease. A place of quiet retreat, the Gardens can be entered from Castle Street or Bridge Street. Francis Gibson, who created them in the 1840s, planted magnificent trees, a pretty rose garden and another in the Dutch style to be viewed from a railed platform, sweeping lawns with statues and arbours.

Adjoining the Gardens are the Anglo-American Memorial Playing Fields created jointly in 1945 by the 65th Fighter Wing of the U.S.A.A.F. and the townspeople as a war memorial. Cricket and hockey pitches overlook the little curved apse where the plaques record the names of the fallen.

The mystery of the Battle Ditches has been a challenge to archaeologists for many years. Professional excavations to date have established them as Saxon and also that they encompassed the town in early times. Certainly the alternative name on old maps of 'Paille' or 'Pessel' Ditches is a likely corruption of palisade for defensive purposes.

Beyond the approach to the Ditches in Abbey Lane are the ironwork gates leading into Audley End Park. A short stroll on the upward path soon reveals the copper turrets of the Mansion.

Bridge End Gardens

THE MARKET PLACE

The Market Place, heart of the town since Geoffrey De Mandeville transferred the market from Newport in 1141, was almost wiped clean of its history in the 19th century. It had witnessed the burning of a Marian martyr; here bulls were lawfully baited until at least 1712 when 'five shillings was paid for a new bull ring and collar'; a Cockpit sunk near the Town Malt Mill; whipping post and the stocks close by the old Market Cross. Cattle and horses thronged the square on market days. All these were cleared away for the newly planned Market Place.

The most dramatic change was the building in 1848 of the Corn Exchange which replaced the Woolstaplers Hall, the agriculture of the district having gradually changed from sheep to grain. Designed by Robert Tress, it represented the ambition and civic pride of the Victorians who while sternly practical saw nothing untoward in planting what Pevsner calls 'a building in a jolly and tasteless Italian style' in an ancient English market town, although acknowledging the Woolstaplers Hall by placing a symbolic ram's head over the main entrance.

Today, although barley and wheat still dominate our agriculture, farmers have long since ceased the practice of bringing in their samples of grain to the corn merchants and since 1975 the ingeniously converted building has become a busy county library and arts centre, winning a national award for the way the design has catered for the disabled. The Corn Exchange has also been connected on three floors with the old Town Library, built at the same time. The library, which has been serving the town since 1832, is now under the trusteeship of the County and functions as a Centre for Victorian Studies and Local History and has many treasures among its 18,000 books. Of special importance is the large collection of works on Natural History bequeathed by George Stacey Gibson, an eminent botanist, who wrote the first *Flora of Essex* in 1862. The books are housed in their original fine mahogany bookcases and are frequently exhibited. He was in fact the great benefactor of the Town Library.

Market Day

Town Hall

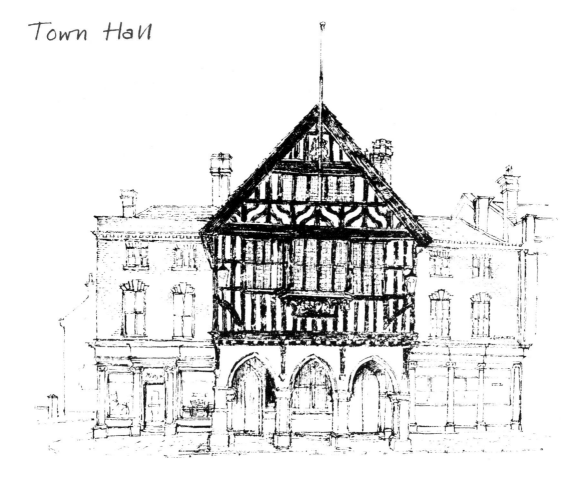

Thirty years after the arresting novelty of the Corn Exchange, a new Town Hall was built behind the austere red brick façade of 1762. The architect, Edward Burgess, turned back the clock with his imposing entrance, more magnificently Tudor than any 16th century building in the town. Standing astride the pavement it provides a fine background for all occasions of civic or national importance. The building was yet another gift of George Stacey Gibson, for at that time this Quaker family of maltsters and bankers was the most influential in the town.

Also reminiscent of red brick Tudor architecture is the handsome building of Barclay's Bank designed by Eden Nesfield in 1874, and originally Gibson's Bank. The Tukes through marriage with the Gibsons became directors of their bank, and the Tukes' close association with it to this day has enabled the town to feel that here Barclays Bank first truly flourished.

The more modest Georgian building on the North side has a charming Regency verandah overlooking the busy market below. This was originally the home and business of John Emson, and the jolly, carved head over the side entrance – which incidentally leads to a beautiful staircase – is reputed to be his. His sons recorded in their writings different aspects of the town's life. Charles translated the Cartulary of Walden Abbey, upon whose site Audley End Mansion stands; Edmund transcribed all the early documents in the Corporation Archives into six indexed volumes. Frank wrote his own history of the town and as if to lighten the subject such books as *The Comick*

History of Saffron Walden and *Our Town: Life at Slowborough*, both full of Victorian puns and nonsense!

The final seal of Victorian respectability in the Market Place was the erection of the Drinking Fountain – again a Gibson presentation to celebrate the wedding of an earlier Prince of Wales to Princess Alexandra in 1863. The fountain was brought from the London Exhibition of 1862. It was a proud centrepiece with its scriptural carvings but after a hundred years in the market became shabby and neglected, to be affectionately restored in 1975 by a generation with a fresh appraisal of Victoriana. The young designer, John Bentley, was later responsible for the Roman Catholic Cathedral at Westminster.

Market Place

A portrait of John Emson above his own front door?

John Emson
Market Hill

The Cockpit off Market Hill marks the entrance to the arena where this form of sport was carried on. The old iron railing for spectators has disappeared. On the plastered wall can be seen several examples of pargetting designs specially executed for a recent TV programme.

The Cockpit

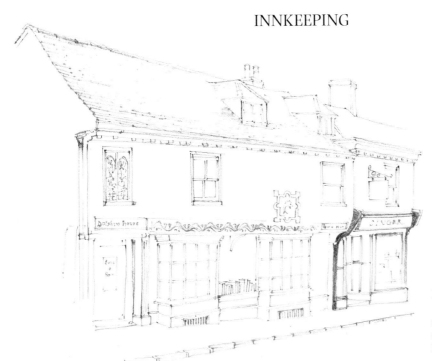

Below the *Dolphin* inn sign on this 17th century house is the bressummer beam faced with a richly ornamental plaster work continuing the dolphin motif.

Dolphin House

Saffron Walden, because of its surrounding hills, was never a main coach route, although the so-called 'Fly' called daily on its way between Cambridge and London. However, in a busy market town the hostelry with its food, drink and good stabling was an intrinsic part of life, and Walden was rich in inns of all kinds; there were seventeen in 1786 when the population was just over 3,000, whereas today, nearing 12,000 there are only about fourteen.

In Elizabethan times there was a tendency to turn dwelling houses into inns such as the celebrated *Angel*, *The Bell* and *The Black Boy*, all round the hub of the market and all long since gone. Today an old inn is often converted into a house of great character.

Attempting to trace their history through name or position resembles a game of General Post. They moved from street to street as *The Cross Keys*, *The Waggon and Horses* and *The Eight Bells* have done, though all now still thriving. Sometimes the Inns changed their names – *The King's Arms* in Market Hill was *The Plow* in 1734 and before that *The Post Horse*. Or became shops like *The Dolphin* in Gold Street, still with its original sign embedded in the plaster. *The Greyhound* in the High Street is now *The Weekly News* office, and the ancient *Hoops* a recent conversion to a *Le Routier* restaurant, and shops. Only the steadfast *White Horse* near the Town Hall has kept both name and position since 1687.

That *The White Hart* in the High Street did not survive is to be regretted for here Samuel Pepys enjoyed his profitable visit. The early 19th century building that replaced it was school, Wartime Emergency Depot and County Library before attaining its present status as Magistrates Court and Registry Office.

Pargetting tool

Pargetting - Sun Inn
Tom Hickathrift & the
Wisbech Giant

Pargetting - Sun Inn

SUN INN. At each corner of the small cross roads on Market Hill are medieval buildings that have scarcely altered over the centuries. The group of four still known collectively as *The Sun Inn* are the most photographed in the town, and have an air of fantasy with their oversailing gables of varied size, a massive door and the lively pargetting and decoration of different periods that enrich the entire frontage. There are birds and foliage, horseshoes and geometrical patterns and a mysterious leg that may have been a trade sign.

The outstanding plaster bas relief illustrated here represents the old East Anglian legend of the fight between the Wisbech giant and Tom Hickathrift, a young carter of such incredible strength that he could lift a haystack on his fork. Legend says that Tom defeated the giant with his axletree, using his cartwheel as a shield. Their costumes are of the 17th century at a time when *The Sun* acquired its own story. Did Cromwell really lodge at the inn when holding his meetings in the church opposite? Although it is possible, the discovery of tiles bearing his likeness is the only fact to lend credence to the story.

The White Horse

This dignified building capped with a mansard roof replaced in the early 19th century *The White Horse* of 1689. Rather less formal is the rear with the mixture of weather-boarding, plaster and timber framing.

Built as a private house in the 16th century, the façade retains many of its original features. The roughcast panels are a 20th century renovation, but the moulded bressummer beam with its foliated decoration and the casement windows on both floors are original. The inn's name was moved from Hill Street in the 1840s during alterations to the Borough Market.

The Eight Bens

The Cross Keys Hotel

It will be observed that the roof of this 16th century inn was raised sometime in the 18th century but the extra weight would be easily borne by the sturdy jettied upper storey. The attractive traceried windows on the ground floor are not so ancient as they appear.

Three houses, all of 16th century origin, altered and refaced in the 17th and 18th centuries, have since the last War been connected to form the main hotel of the town without losing their character.

The Saffron Hotel

No record of the inns of this market town could be complete without a special tribute to the most celebrated of them all – *The Rose and Crown* in the Market Place, destroyed in a tragic fire on Christmas Night, 1969. Its loss still lies heavily on the hearts of people for the old building had played a notable part in the life of the town since the days when the Woolcombers had ended their procession with a feast at *The Rose*. Here generations of farmers gathered on Market Day, here the 18th century steward of Audley End, Thomas Pennystone, collected tithes annually from the tenants over a beef and ale dinner; here the old post chaise would start and, later, the railway bus would deliver passengers after labouring up the hills from the distant station; and here was the favourite hotel of American Airmen in World War II. The carved bunch of grapes suspended over Boots' shop is a pathetic reminder of the original entrance. Should it ever be proved that William Shakespeare was one of his Company of King's Players when they performed in the spacious cobbled Yard of *The Rose* in 1606, that would indeed be a most worthy memorial.

Bunch of Grapes - Boots

Dobson's & Williams - King St.

A late 15th century hall house in King Street, the only structural alteration being the addition of an upper storey to the central 'hall'.

THE ROWS

The original medieval shop windows in Cross Street.

'The Rows', narrow traders' lanes running parallel to King Street towards the Market Place and intersected by cross streets, are a remarkable and rare medieval survival. Each of the Rows had its particular traders – Fish Hill, Tanners, Drapers, Mercers, Butchers Row, and so on. They were originally mere stalls, slowly developing into shops, even with living quarters above.

In the narrow opening to Cross Street by *The Hoops* can be seen on each side windows that were characteristic of the Rows. Then they were mere shuttered openings, the shutters being lowered to make counters. Another Dragon post graces this corner.

The Rows have decreased slightly due to road widening (that was when little Creep Mouse Alley disappeared) or been shortened by building development, but the pattern is still well marked. They became more nondescript during the 19th century when larger shops round the Market were opened. Today, with banks, estate agents and other commercial buildings dominating the Market Place, the old Rows are experiencing a revival as intimate little shops grow in popularity.

Mercers Row.

THE 'PEPYS' MAZER BOWL

From Pepys Diary, February 27th, 1660
'. . . took horse straight to Saffron Walden where at The White Hart we set up our horses and took the master of the house to show us Audley End House . . . in which the stateliness of ceilings, chimney-pieces, and form of the whole was exceedingly worth seeing. He took us into the cellar where we drank most admirable drink, a health to the King. Here I played on my flageolette, there being an excellent echo . . . In our going, my landlord carried us through a very old hospital or almshouse where forty poor people were maintained . . . They brought me a draft of their drink in a brown bowl tipt with silver which I drank off, and at the bottom was a picture of the Virgin and the child in her arms, done in silver . . .'

ALMSHOUSES

The earliest almshouse 'in sustenation of 13 poor men and women' was built in 1400 on the orchard of Roger De Walden, Archbishop of Canterbury in 1397. Those now grouped in Park Lane and Abbey Lane are the replacements and extensions of the original. An ancient brass plate preserved in the present Trustees' Room commemorates Thomas Byrd 'out of whose goods this fire-hearth was erected' and his family.

The 'Pepys' Mazer Bowl was a treasure possessed by the trustees for nearly 400 years. A modest little bowl, less than 8 inches in diameter, it bore the silver mark for the year 1507/8, and in appearance was just as Pepys described it. It was probably intended for religious purposes when presented by Margaret Bergchman (Bridgeman), but tradition gave it only ceremonial usage.

In the 1920s urgent repairs were needed to the roof of the almshouses and after local and many national protests it was auctioned at Christie's for £2,900, its destination inevitably the United States. There it remained in the Pierpont Morgan Library until 1971 when it was brought to England and again sold at Christie's this time for £22,000. The mazer is now in a private collection in Sussex, its sale still regretted by the town and its value diminished by the separation from its original home. A replica can be seen in the Museum, and excellent photographs of the original are in the Town Library.

Today, Walden's almshouses are being modernised into comfortable homes. There is also ample sheltered housing in purpose built flats and bungalows or converted large houses, maintaining this ancient traditional care for the elderly. The town was provided with its own general hospital as early as 1866 through the generosity of the Gibsons, and its sale by the N.H.S. was deplored by all Waldenians.

King Edward VI's Almshouses in Abbey Lane after they were rebuilt in 1834.

THE CHURCH – AND DISSENTERS

The majestic Church of St. Mary the Virgin is immediately impressive; among the townsfolk its presence has inspired deep affection even when they have rebelled against its teaching. In successive centuries from Norman times it has been built and rebuilt, yet something of the work of every generation has always survived.

The church as we see it today was built in the fifty years between 1475 and 1525 and the work was achieved in great measure by the devotion and exertions of John Leche who was vicar during most of that time, and his sister Dame Joane Bradbury, widow of a Lord Mayor of London. In addition to their own financial help they received gifts from such people as King Henry VII, who presented a hundred oaks from the Forest of Chesterford.

In this way the church attained the splendour of many of the great wool churches, and the colours of its painted walls, stained glass, rich carpets, hangings and vestments, its gold and silver plate, provided a fine setting for processions, pageants and the Mystery Plays of that period. This glory with all the ancient ceremonial disappeared at the Reformation and the links with the nearby Walden Abbey to which the De Mandevilles had presented the church's revenues in 1130 were severed. Instead, these were granted by King Henry VIII to his Chancellor, Lord Audley, thereby opening the first page of Audley End's history.

The church suffered further depredations during the Civil War although it is unlikely that meetings held by Cromwell and General Fairfax in 'the greate churche' in 1647 occasioned deliberate defacement. The really severe structural damage happened when it was struck by lightning in 1769; this split the body of the church and broke the windows. There followed a time of some decay until a great three-year work of restoration was begun in 1790 which brought new life to the church but swept away many medieval features.

When there were plans in 1830 to erect the present graceful spire the community responded readily, and the Vicar's appeal to an old Quaker, Wyatt George Gibson, for a contribution is a familiar story and a measure of the unity of affection for the ancient building. The Quaker whose Meeting had resisted the church's authority for 150 years refused on principle to contribute: 'Thee expects a Quaker to give money for a new steeple? Indeed, I will not' – then after a pause – 'But I'll give thee £300 to pull down the old one'. So honour was satisfied. The irony was that the spire was designed by the eminent church architect of the day. Thomas Rickman, himself a Quaker.

Once more, through the 1970s, the vast sum of nearly a quarter of a million has been raised for a much needed restoration of the tower and spire. To celebrate the completion of repairs Great Ringing Day, a custom dating back to 1642 was again held in 1981 after a lapse of seven years. Today, the interior of the church may lack the original medieval splendour, but its lofty arches and its clear light have austere dignity equally beautiful.

THE CATHOLICS have been housed since 1906 in a fine converted barn in Castle Street, once part of the ancient 'Close' when the building was occupied by priests in the reign of Mary Tudor. Today the church shares in this unusually united community.

THE DISSENTERS. The burning of John Bradford at Smithfield in 1555 was an inspiration to the Dissenters in Walden. Bradford had often ministered and preached in the town and had many loyal followers; so strong were the feelings aroused by his martyrdom that to deter these people another preacher, John Newman, a pewterer from Kent, was brought to Walden to suffer the same fate. On the martyrdom of both these men, the Baptists and Congregationalists founded their own church. In the 19th century the Methodists courageously built their chapel in Castle Street, then the toughest area in the town.

The Quakers, originally the most persecuted of all the Dissenters, still gather at the same place in the High Street where they first met in 1676, in a Meeting House, built and rebuilt as needed.

Up to the first quarter of this century there were nine active non-conformists chapels and meeting houses. One is now a builder's business, one an educational centre, one a private house. The others continue to thrive with a strong congregational spirit in the tradition of the town.

St Mary the Virgin

This austere building of 1811 with its Ionic four-column portico replaced the original church of 1694, which in turn was built on the site of the barn where the congregation first worshipped. The elegant mahogany pulpit with its swept staircase is of fine late 18th century craftsmanship.

This chapel was also built on the site of the barn in 1865 where the worshippers had gathered since 1823. Two women preachers, Miss Berger and Mrs Webster founded the chapel in spite of strong opposition to their sex.

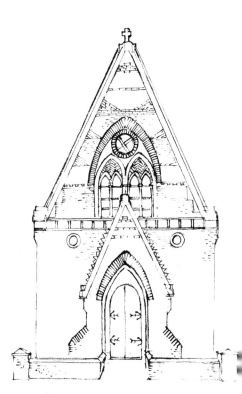

Facade . Methodist Church

A TRADITION OF LEARNING

Friend's School

The tradition of education in Saffron Walden owes much to the vision and endeavours of individual persons. As early as 1317 there is mention in the Cartulary of Walden Abbey of one, Reginald, 'scholemaster of Walden'; and priests serving at the Church 'might receive one son of each inhabitant to instruct in the alphabet and graces', but this brought little real education to the town. It was due to the resourcefulness of two early Tudor women – Dame Joane Bradbury and to a lesser extent Dame Katherine Semar – that Saffron Walden Grammar School opened in 1525

The old schoolroom in Castle Street still survives, and a door leading into a garden retains the lettering: AUT DISCE, AUT DOCE, AUT DISCEDE, Learn, teach or leave!

In 1881 a fine new building was erected in Ashdon Road, but the life of the Grammar School ended in 1940 when it was requisitioned by the R.A.F. and later by the U.S.A.A.F., to flourish again

now as the Dame Bradbury Preparatory School. Dame Katherine Semar is also commemorated in a new Junior School.

Education was a primary concern of 19th century Quakers in the town, especially of George Stacey Gibson. In the last years of his life he fulfilled two long-held desires – the building of a co-educational Friends School in 1879, bringing out an old foundation from the London area, and five years later the adjacent Teacher Training College, both with spacious grounds. The College is now the international Bell College.

A man who also made his vision a reality with the 1944 Education Act was Lord Butler who as 'RAB' represented Walden throughout his long Parliamentary career. It was fitting that the largest Junior School in the town has been named after him. This in turn incorporated the pioneer non-denominational school founded in 1838, the much-loved 'Boys British'.

Saffron Walden Museum

English Glass Posset Pot
circa 1685

In the Museum a more detailed pictorial record of the development of the town and its buildings can be studied. The gallery 'Walden: History in Buildings' shows methods of construction, materials used locally and decorative features especially pargetting. With section of timber framing, windows and door frames, shutters